WHAT CAN HAPPEN SERIES — BY MISS J

WHEN FLYING ON AN AIRPLANE

A Guidebook to events that can take place Before, During, and After taking an Airplane flight
-- 'Miss J' of SpeakToMissJ.com

When Flying on an Airplane

Every effort has been made to ensure that this book contains valuable information that when applied can be useful in everyday life. However, neither the publisher nor author, are engaged in rendering professional advice or services to the individual reader. The ideas, procedures, and suggestions contained in this book are not intended as a substitute for consulting with a medical professional.

All matters regarding your social, physical and mental health should be directed to a qualified practitioner of the healing arts. Neither the author nor publisher shall be liable or responsible or any loss, injury, or damage allegedly arising from any information or suggestions in this book.

The opinions expressed in this book represent the personal views of the author and not the publisher.

When Flying on an Airplane

Amazon.com/author/SpeakToMissJ

What Can Happen Series: When Flying on an Airplane

Miss J – author, speaker, blogger, photographer, business owner and entrepreneur

ThingsYouWantedToSay.com

SpeakToMissJ.com

ISBN: 9798706259921

When Flying on an Airplane

Amazon.com/author/SpeakToMissJ

When I made my first trip to an airport and took that first commercial airplane flight, I was nervous, a little scared, and not sure what to do.

Airports can be overwhelming and confusing if you have never been there before. And it doesn't help that the action movies on TV always show a hijacking or disaster or crash of some kind.

So after taking my first flight and realizing that everything went OK, I took some more flights and found out that this was a MUCH faster and More Convenient way to travel long distances.

This book is for all of those who fly commercial airlines, especially for those who are new to flight.

Airplane travel is safer than driving and once you get used to it, flying has so many benefits.

Safe Travels!

Miss J

This is a Guidebook for Airplane travelers. A Guidebook that is all about the Things That Can Happen on a Plane.

Events that can take place Before, During, and After taking an Airplane flight.

When Flying on an Airplane

1.) Did you know that there are certain vehicles allowed around the airplane, near the runway on the 'backside' of the airport? Luggage vehicles, snack / food trucks, maintenance / fuel vehicles, and more. It's a Giant Dance of Man and Machine working together to get planes in the air.

When Flying on an Airplane

2.)	Did you know that airlines carry dead bodies in the luggage compartment underneath the plane? When a family member needs to get the deceased from one city to another for the burial, the caskets with the dead body are loaded on to the plane privately so the only people that know they are there are the baggage handlers and the family members.

3.)   If you are going somewhere you have never been, you might have a hard time deciding what you are going to wear. You might change the outfit 3 – 7 – 10 times before you decide to just bring several. This often happens when you can't check the weather forecast and get a reliable idea of what it is going to be like when you get there. Since the weather can change last minute! I have packed clothing because the forecast said it would be cold, but then the temperature changed at the last minute and it was hot – so there I was walking around in a sweater, hot as can be, while everybody else had light summer clothing on! And I have also packed too light when it got cold suddenly and I wasn't prepared. My advice is to check the forecast no more than 1 or 2 days out so you have a better idea of what it will be like and can pack the appropriate clothing.

4.)   Before you get on the airplane you have to go thru security. To get there you get in the security line which feels like herding cattle. It is like doing the dance called 'The Slide': to the left, to the left, to the right, to the right, now Slide forward and show ID!! Make sure you have your ID out and have printed your boarding pass. These lines are the longest part of the security process and you need to show up early to make sure you can get thru them in time to get on your plane.

When Flying on an Airplane

5.) Once you have boarded the plane and had a seat, you will notice that there will be some people who have more than the allowed carry-ons and personal items. Some people have no problem breaking the rules. The rules apparently don't apply to them. Don't let this offend you, even though they take up several spaces in the luggage compartment up top with their items alone. They might even put it above you, in 'your' space, instead of placing it above them. Remember, in their mind it is 'their world and you just live in it'. In other words they don't give a hoot about you or anybody else.

6.) When your airplane has landed, you will hear over the intercom to 'remain seated and don't unbuckle' until the airplane has gotten to the gate and come to a stop. Even though it can take 10-20 minutes to get off the plane some people will stand up right away and get in line to make sure they can get off quickly. I said in my mind, 'maybe they have an emergency or are running late for an appointment' so that way I don't view it as rude.

When Flying on an Airplane

7.) When people on the plane see somebody in a rush to get off the plane they can often be heard making rude comments about them – trying to start arguments. If you see this happen, just remember that not everybody was raised with manners, and you don't have to allow their anger to jump on your luggage and go home with you. Let them keep their own bad attitude as a personal item.

8.)	When it is time to take off your shoes and put them on the conveyor belt at security, some people will refuse to obey the rules and argue with security... Just wear shoes that are easy to slip on and off so that way you won't have any problems. Security wants to make sure you aren't hiding something in your shoes – at one time there were people who tried to smuggle weapons, drugs, and other bad things in hidden compartments in the shoes. So now they scan them to make sure nothing is being snuck in.

9.) Security staff usually yell out 'take off your belt, shoes and put purse, cellphone, coins, keys, coats and put them in a tote and on the conveyor belt. Put anything metal and all electronics larger than your phone in a plastic tote and be prepared so you don't have to hold up the line, and you can just walk into the scanner.' Because one person doesn't understand or refuses to take off their shoes and obey TSA's rules, it seems like it rarely flows smoothly. Sometimes if a person has never flown before they are nervous and are not sure what to do and often stop to ask questions which slows down the line. They have an individual looking at the scanner to make sure you are not bringing on a gun or liquid larger than 3oz or anything dangerous. If the scanner detects something that they think is questionable, your bag will be brought over to a separate table and they will ask you questions about the contents and open the bag and go thru it until they are satisfied that it is not dangerous. If you have something that is not allowed as a carryon but is allowed in checked luggage under the plane, then you can get back out of line, go check it in, and then come back thru security a 2nd time – or you can just let them throw it away for you. They will make you throw away drinks, so don't expect to bring your coffee or water with you. But of course, as always, the choice is yours.

10.)   So once you go thru the line, you will put all your carryon and personal items, along with your shoes and anything metal on the conveyor belt to be scanned, then you will step into a glass 'phone booth' and raise your hands above your head while a machine will go around you and scan for metal or anything that looks suspicious. If it sets off an alert - It could be bobby pin, jewelry, watches, earrings, metal screws or plates in your body, etc... so if anything gets there attention you will be asked to step aside where you can be 'patted down' or have a hand held metal detector passed over your body.

11.) Just remember, if there is something that they think is a threat. So don't ever try to take a gun to the airport or any other weapon, because the only people allowed to do so are the police and security. It is not my rules – and that would be a quick way to get yourself arrested.

12.)   Once all goes well in security, you are then free to go pick up your belongings from the totes that came out of the scanner on the conveyor belt – put your shoes back on and go into the airport and go to the gate where you will be able to board your plane.

13.)   Once you are seated on the plane you can hear other people's conversations, you would think they would know to put on their 'quiet voice' but instead they talk loud and you can hear everything being said and all about their life, who they are, where they are coming from and going to, who is going to meet them and what they are going to do when they get there. This is not safe to make all this information so public. So never talk about your personal business on a plane and certainly don't talk loud.

14.)   Before the airplane takes off, you will be asked to put your cellphone in 'airplane mode' which is located in 'settings'. They say it is to keep all the phone signals from interfering with the planes equipment during takeoff. Once the plane has taken off and reached a certain altitude the plane's crew will announce that you can turn on all electronics again.

15.)   Sometimes you can be able to look and see what other people on the plane are watching on their phones, their tablets or on their laptop computers – without leaving your seat. I watched an entire movie with another person even though I didn't know them and I was in a seat that wasn't even near them. I realized that there is very little privacy on an airplane so to solve this I went to a store called Five Below and purchased a 'privacy screen' for my phone so you can only see what is on the phone if you are directly in front of it. If you look at the screen from the side you only see black!! Stores like Five Below are my friend and they can be your friend too.

Amazon.com/author/SpeakToMissJ

16.)	When you first board the plane you will notice that the first several rows of seats only have 2 seats in a row instead of the usual 3. This if for those passengers who paid extra for '1ˢᵗ class', to be in seats that have more legroom and are not as crowded.

Amazon.com/author/SpeakToMissJ

17.)   Next you will see that there are 3 seats in a row on each side. These don't have as much legroom and are comfortable unless you have bigger people in the seats around you – because the seats are not set apart from each other – they are built one right up against the next. So you might have to bump elbows with your neighbor.

18.)   Most airlines will assign seats, so that when you are paying for your fare, they will offer you the option to pay more $ to get 'better' seats – such as buying a ticket for 'first class'. If you pay for 'first class' you will be right behind the pilot (there is a limited amount of seats available) have more space and more comfortable seating, and will be served better food (if that is offered on the flight) and you can get off the plane before everybody else does. Some people have no problem paying the extra fare so they can be more comfortable, but you won't get to your destination any sooner.

19.)   If you don't purchase the higher 'first class' ticket, you will be sitting in 'economy' and will be in the middle or back of the plane. You will never know who will be sitting right up on you, in the seats next to you. They might smell good or they might fart a lot, you just never know. This is why some pay more so they have some space between them and the next person.

20.)   Airlines will have 2-3 bathrooms. Always located in the very front or very back of the plane. They are typically very small with barely enough room to turn around. You can only use them when the seatbelt sign has been turned off and you are allowed to stand up.

21.)   When you are in your seat, if you look up you will see 3 small circles above your head. These are small little fans blowing air conditioning down onto the seats below them. Each seat gets its own fan. You can reach up and turn them on or off and direct them to blow on your face or body.

22.)   Next to the fans will be 3 lights, again 1 for each seat. You have your own personal light. You can turn it on and it will shine directly down upon you – so you can read a book during a night flight and not shine the light on anybody else.

23.)   Above your head will also be a button to call the stewardess. This will turn on a light and notify the stewardess so they can come to you. This is meant for you to be able to ask for assistance, help with an emergency, get a blanket or earphones, ask for water, etc... The stewardess job is to help to make the flight more comfortable for you if possible.

24.)   When the airplane is taking off you will be asked to remain seated, with the seatbelt on, until the airplane has reached a certain height, then they will announce over the intercom that it is okay to take off the seatbelt and go to the restroom. Other than going to the bathroom they say to remain seated in your seatbelt for safety sake just in case the plane flies thru any turbulence that shakes the plane.

25.)   Before your plane takes off there is a machine in front of the plane that will push it back away from the gate and there will be people standing outside with a flag directing the pilot which way to turn. In other words, I don't think the plane has a 'reverse' on it. Because the plane is so high you may not be able to see the vehicle that is doing the pushing on your plane, but if you look out the window at the other planes you can see it pushing those planes, so now you will know what it looks like. So they push it back and turn it the right way so the pilot can turn on the engines and drive it forward until it takes off.

26.)   When the plane has landed, there will be a man or woman standing outside with flags or light sticks waving to the pilot to direct them to drive the plane into the right lane to go and park at the correct gate.

27.)   On many planes they have an artist put artwork on the side of the plane, wingtips or on the tail to decorate it. I guess they do it to give you something to look at other than the ground or just 'plane' metal!

28.)   When the airplane is taking off, all of the stewardess's will have a seat and buckle up. This is because it is normal for the take off to be bumpy – so don't be scared if it seems a bit rocky at first – that is normal.

29.)   If the flight is long enough, you will be served some sort of refreshment during the middle of the flight. It might be water and a small bag of pretzels or nuts – or you might be able to get soda and juice or purchase an alcoholic beverage. They even put a slogan on the snack to promote the airline. First class gets a better menu to choose from on flights where food is served.

30.)   When the airplane has landed, there is someone who will drive a cart to the plane to remove the luggage off the plane and drive it to the luggage area of the airport. You can then get off the plane and walk to the 'Baggage Area' to pick up your luggage. There will be different conveyor carousel belts with the flight numbers and cities listed above them. There will be an intercom message stating where your bags will end up. Example: if you flew in from New York it will say 'Flight 1234 from New York arriving at Baggage Carousel #2'. This way you don't have to run from carousel to carousel trying to find your bags. It is then your job to watch for your luggage to come out on the belt and pull it off. If you miss it – don't worry – it just keeps going around in a circle over and over again until somebody grabs it.

31.)   You will see that the majority of luggage is black. This can be rather confusing when trying to get your bag instead of someone else's! I suggest you get different color luggage or put a different color carrying strap on it to make sure your bags stand out from the rest, making them easy to spot. Remember there will usually be a lot of people around trying to get their bags and everybody will be in a rush – so the easier it is to spot the better.

32.)   Just remember if for some reason you are delayed in picking up your luggage, don't get upset! You can go to the Baggage Claim office and they will usually have it there. In fact there was one trip when my husband and I forgot that we had brought a smaller bag with us on the return flight and when we went back to the Baggage Claim office, they were able to match his ID with the luggage tag and it was no problem at all to get the bag back.

33.)   Some people will get on the plane with loud music playing disturbing other people. Just remember they think it is their world and everybody else is just living in it. The stewardess will make an announcement to keep music down to avoid disturbing others. If they keep announcing it, they just might be talking about you.

34.)　　There are people who will get on the airplane and be asleep before it even takes off. They apparently planned for this nap ahead of time or needed the break from staying up late packing or getting up earlier than usual to make the flight on time.

35.)   One individual gets up to go the restroom, and then less than a minute later the person sitting next to them gets up to go to the same restroom. Some people think that having sex on an airplane is cool. Knowing that airplane restrooms are so small, I don't even want to think about where they sit or what they have to touch to make sex possible. If they have been in there too long somebody waiting to use the bathroom might knock on the door and they both are in there and have to come out at the same time – how embarrassing!

36.)   People will try to 'hold' or 'block' seats so that they won't have anybody sit next to them on the flight. They only paid for one seat and remember you do have the right to sit there because you bought a ticket also.

37.)   I remember I was on a flight where a man was sitting near the wing, started throwing a temper tantrum about how he had some sort of medical condition and nobody could sit next to him. The stewardess said that he should have paid for first class. He kept throwing a fit and they moved him to first class anyway – so he could sit by himself. I think he was running a con because he was grinning like he won something when they told him he could move. I would not recommend this behavior because if you make a scene on airplanes in today's culture, you can get arrested!

38.)   Did you know that every airplane that takes off has a U.S. Marshall on the plane with a gun – dressed like an everyday person, and taking the flight with you to ensure everybody's safety?!!

39.)   You will also see that some people bringing animals on the flight. They say they are 'emotional support animals'. Some of these pets can be pretty strange. Don't be surprised what you see.

40.)   When your plane has landed you will be getting off the airplane in a different airport with all new people. It may seem like everybody is looking at you – don't be alarmed – they are just looking. After all, if you are waiting a long time for your flight to leave, any opportunity to look at something or someone else is a way to disrupt the boredom, so people coming off a flight is pure entertainment.

41.)   Always arrive to the airport 1-2 hours early. Why? Just in case it takes a long time to get thru security, you will have time to still make it to your plane before it takes off. You never know if there will be people ahead of you who take a really long time to go thru security, or they resist the rules, or try to take something on the plane that they are not allowed to do and cause the line to be held up while there situation is figured out. Remember, even if you are at the airport, but not on the plane, your plane will take off on time without you.

42.)   When you arrive early and have made it thru security, you will be able to walk to your gate and be able to sit in one of the waiting areas. These waiting areas have big windows that allow you to look at all the planes and see the people that work on the planes, handle the luggage, load the planes with snacks, and watch planes take off and land. Pretty cool.

43.)   If there is snow on the ground and is falling heavy on the planes, then your plane may be delayed taking off or have to be de-iced before it can leave. The airport will make sure the weather is safe for planes to fly in before they allow them to take off. And if ice is forming on the planes, the de-icing spray must be put on the entire plane – coating it with a thick liquid that allows the plane to fly without ice forming on any moving parts or sticking to it and weighing it down. Your plane would have to get in line for its de-icing and when it is your turn, it takes between 10-20 minutes to complete.

DELTA
VERSALIFT
ICEMAN 5
FREQ
DI-18939

44.)   If the plane is unable to take off, or in certain circumstances you are unable to take the flight, airlines can give you a voucher and put you up for the night in a hotel so you can catch a flight the next morning. This is one of the reasons why there are usually so many hotels around the airport.

45.)   Did you know that people that work for the airlines get free flights in the form of vouchers called 'buddy passes'? This allows them to take one of the unsold seats on any flight and fly for free. They have to wait until everybody else has boarded and if there is room for them, then they can get on. Sometimes they can even give these passes to family members and friends to use if they want.

46.)   When you get your ticket, it is important to check to see what gate your plane will be at. There will also be large display boards telling Departure Gate #'s, times, flight #'s and cities. You will want to make sure you check your Flight # / City and see what Gate you are supposed to be at. When you get to the gate check to make sure your Flight # / City is posted at that gate. You don't want to be at one gate and they changed which gate your plane would be at, and you have to cross the airport in a very short amount of time to get to the other one before it takes off – some airports are very big and crowded!! If in doubt, ask an airline employee at the gate.

47.)   Did you know you can actually save the check in fee, if you use your computer or phone to go online and check in within 24 hours before the flight takes off? Let's say for example you are flying Southwest airlines. You would go to Southwest's website online. There will be a space to 'Check In'. You type in your confirmation # and last name, enter in the amount of bags you will be taking, and hit 'submit'. Then the screen will show you your boarding passes! You can print them or save them to your phone (screenshot, wallet, bookmark the page, etc...) and you have all the paperwork you need to get on the plane. If you saved it to your phone, when it is time to get on the plane, you will show them the photo from your phone — they can scan it in without needing a paper boarding pass.

48.)   Airports can be very busy and the bathrooms are no exception. Don't be surprised what people leave behind in the toilet!! Some people can bring in luggage, use the bathroom, and walk out like they were just in there to visit friends – they don't flush, they don't wash their hands – they just walk out!

49.)   Just like other forms of public transportation (buses and trains), people will bring babies on the plane. Sometimes the babies will cry during the flight, they can cry from when they get on the plane till they get off the plane. You might think to yourself 'where are the parents? Can somebody take care of this baby's needs?' Just remember that if you think airports are stressful, babies are even more stressed out and the parents are doing their best to cope with it.

50.)   On occasion, you might see someone get kicked off the plane or asked to take a different flight because they have been drinking too much. Remember there are places in the airport where people can drink their liquor or buy it and take with them – since they won't be 'driving' the plane.

51.)   Inside airports there are often several restaurants and gift shops where you can get a meal, a snack or that last minute gift. You will pay more at these shops than you would outside the airport – but that is the point – you aren't outside – you are inside the airport with limited choices and it is more expensive.

52.)   You can't bring outside food / drinks past security into the airport. But you can purchase food and drinks from the airport and bring that on the plane. So finish eating or drinking before you get to the airport to save yourself some money.

53.)   If this is your first time flying, you might be nervous and be afraid that things will fall off the plane and it will crash. Don't worry... these planes are very expensive and they pay a lot of people to check the plane out and make sure it is safe to fly BEFORE it takes off... mechanics and pilots check every part before they take off. If there are any problems or concerns, they have no problem delaying the flight until it is fixed or switching everybody to another plane if necessary. Remember they are in the business of making $$$ and these planes are extremely expensive, they don't want to lose not even one!! Don't believe everything you heard or what you have seen in the movies!

54.)   If you ever have your checked in luggage damaged by the airline baggage handlers, you can go to the baggage claim office and show them the damage. They will sometimes give you a travel voucher to compensate you for the damage or even give you another bag that is similar! You just have to show them damage that would be covered by their policies. Never hurts to ask.

55.)   When purchasing your airline tickets make sure to pay attention to how long the flight takes. You can get flights that go directly there (called Non-Stop) and others have multiple layovers that could take a really long time. Example: I have looked at flights that took 2 hrs to get there and for the same trip there was tickets I could get that would take 11 hours!!! This was because the longer trip included several stops with long waits at each one.

56.)   What is a Non-Stop flight? A Non-Stop flight is a flight that takes off and flies directly to your destination and lands. No detours, No visiting other airports, No multiple stops, No layovers. It is the quickest way to get where you are going. And it is usually the more expensive tickets. The flights that stop at multiple airports are usually less expensive and take longer to get to where you are going.

57.)   What is a Layover? A Layover is when your flight makes a stop at another airport before it continues on to your destination, and you have to get off the plane and wait awhile before getting back on and continuing – or you have to get off the plane and switch to another plane to finish your travels. This waiting time can be 20 minutes up to 6 hours sometimes. You typically don't have the time to leave the airport and come back in through security again (not that you would want to anyway) so if you have layovers bring something to entertain yourself while you wait! Remember: the more stops you have to make, the more layovers, the longer it takes for you to get where you are going.

58.)   If you are looking out the window before you take off and when you land, you can see how the baggage handlers load or take off the luggage from the airplanes – whether on your plane or the plane beside you. They have a short time to get this done and it shows! They just throw the luggage around. They don't handle it carefully – they just grab it and toss it. So if you have anything fragile to take with you – put it in your carry on or personal item and take it with you onboard the plane – so at least that way you know how it will be handled, and if YOU break it… well I guess it's your fault!

59.)   If you are not sitting next to the window, you will have no control of the window shade. They might pull the shades down for the entire trip and you get no view, or they might raise it up but you still will have to look over them to see out the window (they are small windows).

60.)   If you have the window seat you will be able to adjust the shade yourself. You get to decide if you want the shade open or closed. Letting in the light and the view or keeping it out – it's all up to you!

61.)   The more you pay for your tickets, the earlier you book your flights and check in allows you to board the plane sooner and sometimes allow you to pick out better seats. The first ones on are also the first ones off, so the longer it takes you to board, the longer it will take you to get off the plane when you get there.

62.)   They board the planes in a certain order: disabilities/special needs first, Families with babies in car seats, then people who paid more for First Class/Military, then those who paid for Priority boarding, then the rest of the passengers based on when they checked in online (in order based on who was first) and what section of the plane you purchased tickets for. So wait your turn or Pay Extra to get ahead of the line!

63.)   Now Southwest Airlines handle things differently than the others. They have NO assigned seats. So once you are onboard the plane you can pick whatever seat you want to sit in. Window, middle or aisle. The only exception is that First Class is in the front and you must have a First Class ticket for those seats – otherwise the rest of the plane is open. So those that get on first have the whole plane to pick from.

64.)   On some airlines, it used to be that they had a strict 'dress code'... you had to dress 'business casual' no jeans allowed! They have removed that rule now though. The new rules state that if the Airline thinks it is "inappropriate or offensive" they can refuse to allow you on the plane.

65.)   If you are NOT flying Southwest Airlines, and you are on any other airline, you WILL have assigned seats and must sit in the seat # assigned to you.   When you book, make sure you pay attention to what the seat # is, because if you are flying with someone and want to sit next to them, you have to make sure the seat #'s are next to each other. Otherwise they could be sitting anywhere else on the plane. If you call the airline to book – they can help you by letting you know what seats are still available and reserve the seat #'s you want to ensure that you sit next to the people you are travelling with.

66.)   Before the plane takes off, the stewardess will do a 'safety demonstration' in case of an emergency and will show you how to attach the seatbelt, find and put on your life vest, find emergency exits, get your flotation device from under your seat and attach your oxygen mask that will drop down if the plane loses pressure and they tell you if that happens to always put on your mask first before helping someone else. This information is also printed on a pamphlet in the seat pocket in front of you.

67.)   If you choose to sit directly over where the wings attach, you will be responsible for opening the doors over the wings, and stay and help others to get off the plane in case of emergency, and deploying the life rafts. There are usually only 2 seats on that row (so plenty of extra legroom) and you can't sit there unless you are physically capable of opening the doors and willing to help people climb out of the plane onto the wing, in the event of an emergency.

68.)   There will be someone on the intercom to announce what is happening with the plane. If there is turbulence – put on the seatbelt and stay seated (no bathroom breaks), how long the flight will be, whether you get served refreshments or not, that they are getting ready to land, and what the temperature at your destination is.

69.)   When you get off the plane you will not have to worry about getting to a restroom, since there are usually several within close walking distance. And they have regular cleaning crews go through there so they are usually pretty clean.

70.)   Many airports have toilets that flush themselves! If for some reason it doesn't automatically flush when you get up, there is usually a black button you can push that will flush it for you.

71.)   On any flight, the stewardess can be male or female and be nice or have an attitude! I always say just because somebody has a job doesn't necessarily mean that they like it. They have good days and bad days. They are people just like you and me.

72.)   Remember that the stewardesses are there to help you. Example: when they hand out the cups of water, you can ask for the entire can of water and they will bring one for you. Also when you get bags of snacks (pretzels, trail mix, peanuts, etc...), you can usually ask for several and they will be happy to give you some extra.

73.)   Some people are 'frequent flyers' meaning that they take a lot of flights on a regular basis. They usually get some kind of benefits such as earlier boarding. If you plan on doing a lot of flying, check with the different airlines because they each have their own separate programs with perks you can qualify for.

74.)   As a 'Frequent Flyer' some airports provide special lounges that you can go to and get food, charge your phone, watch the TV, and rest. A personal lounge where you can eat free!

75.)   Major Airports often have a lounge for military personnel called the 'U.S.O.' in the terminals or at the main airport building. These are for active duty or retired military to take a break, grab a snack, and relax before their next flight. If you are not military, don't go – you won't get in.

76.) Some airports are so big that they have trains to take you from one side of the airport to another. The larger and busier airports can be confusing. This is why it is important to show up early and ask an airport employee for instructions on how to get where you need to go.

77.)   Also you can look for directions by following the signs that are placed up high near the ceiling to direct you to different gates, terminals, baggage claim, restrooms, and shopping. The bigger and busier the airport the more signs they tend to have. Just look up!

When Flying on an Airplane

78.)   It is important to check the weather for where you are going and dress accordingly. It can be hot when you go to the airport and cold when you get to your destination. Example: I met a couple who had just got married and had the wedding and honeymoon in the Dominican Republic. It was 98*F when they got on the airplane to head home. It was going to be in the 70's when they got to their destination in California. They had a stop in St. Louis and, at the last minute, decided to get off the plane and go crash a wedding of a friend of a friend. It was New Year's Eve and the temperature that evening was -2*F. This couple had dressed for the warm weather, wearing beach clothes, and was unprepared for the 'outdoor' 'winter' wedding and reception!! They experience a 100*F change in temperature and were suffering because of their lack of proper clothing.

When Flying on an Airplane

(by the way... their luggage with the rest of their clothes had continued on to California ahead of them)

79.)   Sometimes your flight can be really cold on the plane and other times it can be really warm. You never know what you will get, so bring a light jacket just in case.

80.)   Larger airports have flat conveyor belts called 'moving sidewalks'. These are helpful if you have to walk a long way to get to another terminal, especially if you have to carry heavy luggage. You just step on them and stand still and they will carry you to the other side. If you decide to walk then it will feel like you are moving fast, almost running, even though you are only moving at a regular pace.

81.)   If you don't meet your pilot when you first get on the plane you can often see them after the plane has landed. They will open the door to the cockpit and you can step in and say 'Hi' and 'Thank You for the safe trip'. Sometimes they will even let you get into the cockpit and take a picture with them!

82.)   When exiting the plane the stewardesses will be standing by and Thank You for flying with them. They are making sure you get off of the plane safely and then do a quick check to make sure nobody left anything behind.

83.)   I always like to tell my stewardess and pilot, when I get off the plane, if I think they did a great job. Too many people wait until funerals to give compliments – I choose to let them know right on the spot. You never know who needs a word of encouragement and you can brighten their day!

84.)   When you are exiting the plane, there will be several people waiting right outside the door for everybody to get off. These people are waiting to sanitize the plane. They don't have much time before the next flight to get the plane cleaned up and ready to go.

85.)   If you are waiting in the airport you will often see pilots and stewardesses, in uniform with luggage, rushing to get home or even to get to another gate to catch their next flight.

86.)   Did you know that you can see someone famous at the airport? They catch flights to. True story. I was on a flight with 'K. Michelle'. I was sitting next to her assistant. They were dressed down and I didn't know who they were until we got off the plane and people were gathered all around them. Of course my daughter spotted them out right away! And my daughters saw 'Big Time Rush' in the airport when they were coming home from Florida. Same scenario – they were dressed down to blend in. She got pictures with them, I didn't. LOL

87.)   Unless the celebrities are Super Duper Rich with their own plane, then they still take the same flights that you and I do. Just usually sitting in First Class. So when you get on the plane, look from side to side and see if you recognize anybody famous!

88.)   Waiting, waiting, Oh how I love waiting! While waiting on your flight to board, you might see some weird things. Example: somebody pacing back and forth in front of a chair – staring at it and arguing with it. Somebody else has a entire picnic going on – making sandwiches, somebody else having rather loud private cellphone conversations that the rest of the airport can listen in on, and more. Sometimes just watching the crowd is entertainment enough.

89.)   Did you know that there can be hackers at the airport? People stealing credit card information by using scanners to get unprotected credit card data. They see it like if you have money to travel than you must have money! Not everybody using a laptop or cellphone is doing the right thing!!

90.)   How do you protect yourself from a hacker trying to steal your credit card data? Well this is how I do it: wrap your credit cards in Aluminum Foil or buy a 'RFID blocker' wallet or purse. Both of these ways stop the machine from scanning your cards and stealing your data.

91.) Just remember, people who are in a wheelchair get to board the plane first. And when the plane lands they will have people who are waiting to help get them off the plane and push them to their next flight or destination. See, airlines take care of people!

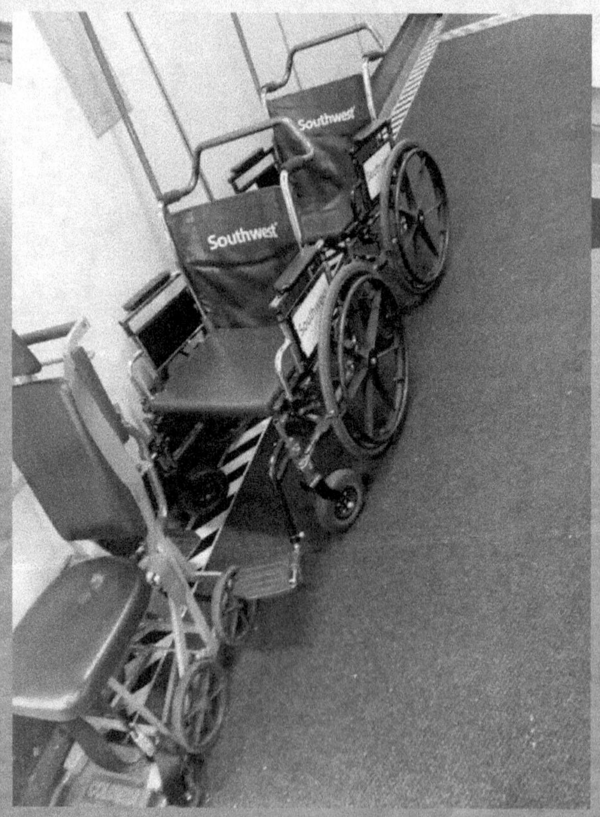

92.)   When people are carrying luggage thru the airport or on the plane, they might bump into you with the bags and may not even realize that they hit you, so they might not even apologize!! So when you see them passing by – just lean over to avoid getting hit.

93.)   Once you have arrived at your destination and are ready to leave the airport there are different exits that will take you to whatever transportation you have chosen to carry you away from the airport. There will be taxi's, UBER, Lyft, Hotel and Car Rental Shuttles, and of course friends and family. If you have arranged for a car rental whose rental lot is outside the airport - Just check the signs and go out the appropriate gate and it will take you to the shuttles that will take you to the rental car location. If the car rental is on the property – just follow the signs to the rental desk.

94.)   I always carry at least $40 in singles, fives and tens. This is so I can tip the UBER, taxi, or shuttle drivers. If they did a good job I give them more, average job gets a couple bucks and horrible job gets nothing at all. I keep this money separate from the rest of my money and keep it handy so I can easily get to it and hand it out without having to dig thru luggage to get it.

95.)   Some cities have more than one airport, so when reserving your rental car online, make sure you select a pickup from the rental that is at the same airport your plane is landing at. It is a big mess to have to pay to catch a ride to across town to get your rental or pay to catch a ride back to the airport from the rental place when you are returning home. Just make sure that your flight and car rental are both at the same airport.

96.)   Some parking lots, rental car places, and hotels only have 1 shuttle bus that waits to get a call from passengers before they will come to the airport. So once you are grabbing your luggage – call them so they can leave to come pick you up and you won't have to wait a long time.

97.)   Shuttle drivers deserve tips. Sometimes the shuttle drivers have to carry very heavy luggage and they might not be very big people. I have seen elderly woman driving the shuttle trying to put heavy luggage on the bus and struggling with it. And some rude people won't even say thank you. So unless they are really rude, I always try to give them a good tip.

98.)   Before you go to any airport, just remember, you must have an official State Issued ID, License or Passport. You can be asked for them several times. So DON'T pack them in your luggage!! Keep them out and Keep them handy.

99.)   When you first walk into the airport you will usually see ticket counters – many airports now have self service kiosks where you can check in, print boarding passes and luggage tags if you have any bags you want to check in to go under the plane. Make sure you put your luggage tags on your luggage before checking them in. Once you do this you and check your bags at the counter then you are free to go get in line to go thru security.

100.)   Travelling light? If you are not checking any bags under the plane, you can check in online – get your boarding passes sent directly to your phone and then skip the luggage line and go straight to the security line. This will speed up the process and makes getting into and out of airports easier since you don't have to mess with any luggage.

101.)   If you plan on taking any luggage with you on your plane flight and having it checked in to be stored under the plane, than make sure you find out what the size limits are for bags. You can usually find them online and they will tell you how big the measurements are that they accept. Anything larger will require that you pay an extra fee which can be expensive. Also there is weight limits for luggage. Most airlines say the weight limit is 50 lbs. And they mean it. If your bag weighs 51 lbs you will be charged a large fee – unless you can unpack it and put some of the weight in other bags. So if you have a scale at home – a bathroom scale is what I use. Weigh your bags before you leave for the airport, that's what I do. I don't like paying extra fees!

102.)   For people that are in the military they have fewer restrictions on luggage – they get to take extra bags for free and they don't worry about the weight – so if you are travelling with military people and they pack light, just have them check your bags in under their name so you don't have to pay any extra fees!

103.)   Carrying any items that security won't let you take on the plane? Example: I was given some expensive shampoo as a gift; however the bottle was too big to be allowed on the plane. You can plan ahead and pack it in your luggage that is going under the plane, or you can do what I did in that example. I asked security if I could write down the person's name that had dropped me off – tape it to the bottle, have security hold it for me and then call that person and have them come back to the airport and pick it up (to ship to me later). This worked great. Now it was also at a smaller airport that wasn't very busy, so I don't know if that would work at a bigger airport. I just didn't want to donate that to security so I have learned to plan ahead and check for what can be carried before I pack.

104.)   Remember to enjoy your flight. One way to do that is look out the windows of the airplane if you get a chance – the view is incredible (in the daytime of course) and since the planes fly very high up in the sky you can look 'down' on clouds from above them – an Unique Perspective you just can't get from the ground!!

When Flying on an Airplane

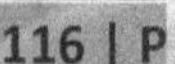

When Flying on an Airplane

105.)   Flying so high allows you to be able to look down and see mountains, rivers, lakes, buildings and vehicles from above – and they look TOTALLY different from that viewpoint! You can even see things that would normally be hidden from your sight.

106.)   Pilots usually announce how high the plane is flying, how fast it is going and how long it will take to get where you are going, and what the local weather is at your destination. Some of the newer and bigger planes have a GPS display on the back of the seat in front of you that will show where the plane is on the map and what you are flying over.

107.)   Some planes have movies and TV shows available on the display screen on the back of the headrest of the chair in front of you. This can be an easy way to pass the time and get to your destination without realizing how long it took!

108.)   Airplanes now have free Wi-Fi that you can connect to, once your plane has reached its cruising height.

109.)   If you need earbuds to listen to the movies – just ask the flight attendant / stewardess. They can get you some for Free!

110.)   If you need to sanitize your seat or armrest – just ask when you are on the airplane because they are quick to get it for you and it is also free.

111.)   Being involved in an argument on a flight can get you in big trouble and cause you to go to jail. Keep this in mind – everybody wasn't raised to be respectful – but they are not worth getting kicked off the plane or going to jail for. So mind your own business and have a safe and peaceful flight.

112.)   You might be on an airplane where someone is constantly passing gas!! If only gas had a color to it and you could find that person and tell them: what did you eat and what restaurant was that?! Don't you dare eat there again!!

113.)   And there is always that lovely person that is sleeping and SNORING loudly the entire flight!! With all these noise distractions – I recommend taking some earphones and listening to your own playlist – of course at a reasonable volume so you don't disturb others!

114.)   Did you know that Active Duty Military have a separate security line they go thru with different rules on the amount of luggage they can take. This makes going thru security very fast for them and they can take extra bags as well.

115.)   Depending on the airport, there are people available who drive small carts that will shuttle you across the airport if you have a disability.

116.)   When your airplane is taking off it has to reach a certain speed before it can get off the ground!! This is the only people I know of that can break the speed limit every day and not get a ticket! LOL So if you are the kind of person who loves fast driving, then airplanes taking off is for you!!

117.)   The airplane flies so high that the change in altitude can cause your ears to 'pop'. What I found works for me is to chew gum. If I don't have any gum I just open and close my mouth as if I had gum and this keeps my ears from popping. Some people say that putting in those foam earplugs works for them... I don't know because I haven't tried that one yet.

118.)   Did you know that the airport has its own fire department in case of an emergency on the scene?

119.)   Did you know also that the airport has its own medical staff?

120.)   Did you know that the airplanes use a 'parking lot' to park planes just like cars do?

121.)   Did you know that some airplanes have charging ports in the seats so you can charge up your mobile phone?   And some even have them in the waiting areas outside the gate before you get on the plane?

122.)   Did you know that even the napkins served on airplanes have their names on them? They are huge promoters of themselves.

123.)   Depending on the size and series # of the plane they can have between 2 to 8 exit doors? Example: an 800 series has 8 exits!

124.)   If you look above your head you will see a button with a symbol that looks like a person with their arms above their heads and it is blue. This is the 'call button' and if you push it, one of the flight attendants will come over to assist you.

125.)   How are the windows on the airplane cleaned on the inside or outside of the plane? If you look closely, you may just see fingerprints!

126.)   Did you know that the flight attendants will be wearing uniforms that have the colors and logo of the airline that they are working for?

127.)   Did you know that when it is foggy or bad weather outside the airplane still has to land safely, and they use different guides to do that? Airplane pilots see the same fog and rain/snow that you do when you drive. Pilots use the airports lights and electronic equipment on the plane to 'see' thru the weather.

128.)   When the main lights inside the airplane are turned off (during night flights) you will see small indirect lighting guiding you to the exits and bathrooms (usually blue led lights – kinda like what you see in some movie theaters).

129.)　Once onboard the plane you have to find your seat. On your ticket it will say your seat # like this: the # of the row first, then the Letter of the seat next. Example: 18C This means your seat is in row 18 and the seat will be the one labeled C. Each row has a sign above it showing the row # and the order of the seats by letter. Typically 3 seats to each side, so A, B, C on one side and D, E, F on the other. Seats A and F will be the window seats usually and C and D will be the aisle.

Amazon.com/author/SpeakToMissJ

Thanks for Reading and Safe
Flying!!
Check out More Books to
come!
Love y'all Sugar!
Miss J

<u>Stay in Touch With Miss J @</u>
SpeakToMissJ.com
ThingsYouWantedToSay.com

<u>Read other Books by Miss J @:</u>
Amazon.com/author/SpeakToMissJ

<u>Follow Miss J on Facebook:</u>
FB: @SpeakToMissJToday